*Acting Edition*

MW01003950

# English

by Sanaz Toossi

### FOR PRODUCTION INQUIRIES

UNITED STATES AND CANADA
info@concordtheatricals.com
1-866-979-0447

UNITED KINGDOM AND EUROPE
licensing@concordtheatricals.co.uk
020-7054-7298

Each title is subject to availability from Concord Theatricals Corp., depending upon country of performance. Please be aware that *ENGLISH* may not be licensed by Concord Theatricals Corp. in your territory. Professional and amateur producers should contact the nearest Concord Theatricals Corp. office or licensing partner to verify availability.

No one shall make any changes in this title(s) for the purpose of production. No part of this book may be reproduced, stored in a retrieval system, scanned, uploaded, or transmitted in any form, by any means, now known or yet to be invented, including mechanical, electronic, digital, photocopying, recording, videotaping, or otherwise, without the prior written permission of the publisher. No one shall share this title(s), or any part of this title(s), through any social media or file hosting websites.

For all inquiries regarding motion picture, television, online/digital and other media rights, please contact Concord Theatricals Corp.

## MUSIC AND THIRD-PARTY MATERIALS USE NOTE

Licensees are solely responsible for obtaining formal written permission from copyright owners to use copyrighted music and/or other copyrighted third-party materials (e.g., artworks, logos) in the performance of this play and are strongly cautioned to do so. If no such permission is obtained by the licensee, then the licensee must use only original music and materials that the licensee owns and controls. Licensees are solely responsible and liable for clearances of all third-party copyrighted materials, including without limitation music, and shall indemnify the copyright owners of the play(s) and their licensing agent, Concord Theatricals Corp., against any costs, expenses, losses and liabilities arising from the use of such copyrighted third-party materials by licensees. For music, please contact the appropriate music licensing authority in your territory for the rights to any incidental music.

## IMPORTANT BILLING AND CREDIT REQUIREMENTS

If you have obtained performance rights to this title, please refer to your licensing agreement for important billing and credit requirements.

*ENGLISH* was co-produced by the Atlantic Theater Company (Neil Pepe, Artistic Director; Jeffory Lawson, Managing Director) and Roundabout Theatre Company (Todd Haimes, Artistic Director; Julia C. Levy, Executive Director; Jill Rafson, Associate Artistic Director), and premiered at the Linda Gross Theater in New York on February 22, 2022. The performance was directed by Knud Adams, with scenic design by Marsha Ginsberg, costume design by Enver Chakartash, lighting design by Reza Behjat, and sound design by Sinan Refik Zafar. The Production Stage Manager was Alex H. Hajjar, and the Assistant Stage Manager was Gracie Carleton. The cast was as follows:

**MARJAN**. . . . . . . . . . . . . . . . . . . . . . . . . . . . . . . . . . . . . . . . . . . Marjan Neshat

**ELHAM** . . . . . . . . . . . . . . . . . . . . . . . . . . . . . . . . . . . . . . . . . . . Tala Ashe

**ROYA** . . . . . . . . . . . . . . . . . . . . . . . . . . . . . . . . . . . . . . . . . . . Pooya Mohseni

**OMID**. . . . . . . . . . . . . . . . . . . . . . . . . . . . . . . . . . . . . . . . . . . .Hadi Tabbal

**GOLI**. . . . . . . . . . . . . . . . . . . . . . . . . . . . . . . . . . . . . . . . . . .Ava Lalezarzadeh

# CHARACTERS

**MARJAN** – the teacher; 44; light accent; was taught American English
**ELHAM** – a student; 28; very thick accent; bulldozes through English
**ROYA** – a student; 54; thick accent
**OMID** – a student; 29; barely detectable accent
**GOLI** – a student; 18; light, sweet accent

# SETTING

2008. Karaj, Iran.

# ON LANGUAGE

This play, with a brief noted exception, will be heard in English.

**Bolded dialogue** signifies that a character is speaking English. Nonbolded dialogue signifies that a character is speaking Farsi.

In the world of the play, when a character is speaking English, the audience will be hearing accented English. In the world of the play, when a character is speaking Farsi, the audience will be hearing unaccented English.

For the most part, I have not written out pronunciation. Certain sounds give Farsi speakers a hard time, the most prominent troublemaker being the "w" sound. *Water* might become *vater* if the speaker is not careful. Or especially if they're careful.

Interruptions are denoted with a forward slash.

[Dialogue in brackets] is to be communicated nonverbally, sometimes because the character does not know the word in English, but not always.

Marjan comes in with corrections on <u>underlined lines</u>.

## Prologue

*(2008. Karaj, Iran.)*

*(A windowed classroom with a whiteboard, TV, and a desk on which a boombox sits.)*

*(On the chalkboard, in lovely handwriting, is written:* TOEFL: Test of English as a Foreign Language.*)*

*(***MARJAN*** writes a directive:* English Only. *She underlines it.)*

## Week 1: Monday

*(**GOLI** stands at the front of the class, holding a small eyebrow pencil.)*

**GOLI.** So I'm starting now – I should start now, right?

**MARJAN. Whenever you're ready, darling.**

**GOLI.** In English, yeah right?

**MARJAN. English always.**

**GOLI.** Okay. Okay! I'll do my best? I'll – Okay: **Hello, my name is Goli.**

| ROYA. | ELHAM. | OMID. | MARJAN. |
|---|---|---|---|
| Hello, Goli | Hello | Hi | Hello, Goli! |

**GOLI.** Oh oh wait actually nosorry hold on –

**In the paper**

**In the paper with the names**

**The paper with the names says my name is Golnaz**

**Golnaz is my real name**

**MARJAN. Which name do you prefer?**

**GOLI. I do not prefer.**

**MARJAN. May we call you Golnaz?**

**GOLI.** Golnaz is totally great.

**MARJAN. English, Golnaz. I know it's tricky at first.**

**GOLI. I am very sorry.**

**MARJAN. You'll get it in no time. What did you bring in for show and tell?**

**GOLI. Yes.**

**What?**

**MARJAN.** Show and tell – did you bring something in for show and tell –

**GOLI.** Excuse me sorry I like Goli for name for me.

**MARJAN.** Goli it is. No problem. What do you have there?

**GOLI.** Okay, so I – English okay here I go –

*(Holds up an eyebrow pencil.)*

This is pencil

Pencil for eyebrow

I want [thick, glam] big eyebrow but I take too much hair when I am young

This pencil is for make not real hairs

You do like *(She haphazardly fills in one of her eyebrows.)*

Uh. Okay.

This is not good I need mirror

**MARJAN.** You need *a* mirror.

**GOLI.** I need a mirror oh my god this is super boring I'm so sorry

**MARJAN.** No no you are doing so well –

**GOLI.** I thought it'd be cool for some reason to show everyone how to fill in their brows. Because brows are really so important and what if you don't have a mirror? Like what if you're in the car? But to be honest I don't think I can even do it without a mirror.

**MARJAN.** Don't be sorry! We were speaking English with eachother.

I think it's one of the greatest things two people can do together.

**MARJAN.** Thank you, Goli, for speaking English with me.

Now continue.

**GOLI.** I am... I sound...

I don't um I don't know how to say it in English?

**MARJAN.** I for one think it's nice that you can't insult yourself in English.

Take your time. You are more than capable of expressing yourself.

*(Beat.)*

**GOLI.** I like English very much.

When I am little, I like English.

I want to speak English.

Before I speak Farsi good, I know I want to speak English.

**MARJAN.** What do you like about it?

**GOLI.** English does not want to be poetry like Farsi.

It is like some rice. English is the rice.

You take some rice and you make the rice whatever you want.

It tries not – What is the word for goes to bottom of water?

**MARJAN.** Sink.

**GOLI.** Thank you. Yes.

English. English does not try to sink or get out of water.

English it stays on top of water...it only wants to [bob on the water; stay afloat]

**MARJAN.** I couldn't agree with you more.

## Week 1: Wednesday

(**ROYA** *and* **ELHAM** *stand at the front of the class.*)

**ELHAM.** Hello what is it your favorite color?

**ROYA.** It is red my favorite color.

**ELHAM.** Red it is...strong. Strong color. Very strong.

**ROYA.** Very strong. It is strong. I am strong.

One time I carry six boxes.

**ELHAM.** Okay. Wow. Six.

**ROYA.** One time big chair. Big big chair.

*(Beat.)*

**ELHAM.** It is over now.

**MARJAN.** Keep going! What a fascinating conversation.

**ELHAM.** Yes. This is. Scintillating conversation.

**MARJAN.** Let's try role-playing.

**ELHAM.** What is that –

**MARJAN.** English, Elham.

**ELHAM.** What is it rolling play? Is it on test?

**MARJAN.** Role play is when you pretend to be someone else.

**ELHAM.** Oh.

**MARJAN.** Actually. Has anyone taken the test before?

*(No one raises their hand.)*

Oh, good! Good. Alright. Why do we learn language? What do you think, Goli? Why do we learn language?

**GOLI**. Um. To say if we are hungry.

**MARJAN**. Yes! To speak our needs. Why else?

   *(Beat.)*

**OMID**. To bring the inside to the outside.

**MARJAN**. Yes. To speak not only our needs but our wants. To speak our souls. To *speak*. And to... *(Motions at her ear.)* listen. To the insides of others.

We're just having a conversation. You speak. You listen. This is just life! Remember that, and the TOEFL will feel less like a test.

   *(Beat.)*

Alright. Elham, have a conversation with Roya pretending to be...Christiane Amanpour. Go ahead, ladies. I won't correct you too much. Interview your guest, Christiane.

**ELHAM**. Very good okay. Roya, where do you live?

**ROYA**. I live in the Canada.

**ELHAM**. No. Here is Iran.

**ROYA**. Yes. Of course.

**ELHAM**. You do live here.

**ROYA**. No.

**ELHAM**. You do not live here?

**ROYA**. Nader is my son.

**ELHAM**. Roya, you're not answering my question.

**MARJAN**. English, Elham.

**ELHAM**. Roya. Where. Do you. Live.

**ROYA**. Canada.

**ELHAM**. Okay. I'm not quite sure what's happening.

**MARJAN.** Roya, why don't you go ahead and ask Elham a few questions.

**ELHAM.** No I can do I can do. Roya why you are like this –

**ROYA.** You do not ask so I tell you now. My son Nader lives in <u>the Canada</u> [**MARJAN.** Canada]. I have permanent resident card.

**ELHAM.** Wait wait if you have permanent resident card what you do in class? Go to Canada.

**ROYA.** Nader has daughter Claire.

Claire is the granddaughter of me <u>mine</u> [**MARJAN.** my granddaughter] my granddaughter.

Nader and the wife want I speak in English with Claire.

So here is Roya in class.

**MARJAN.** What a gift you are giving this girl: learning a new language so that you can know her fully. Elham, what do you think?

**ELHAM.** I think...very good for Claire.

**MARJAN.** I'm sure you have more to say! You're a woman of many opinions. It's a simple conversation.

**ELHAM.** It is like feeling – I think – This is unnatural.

**MARJAN.** Why?

**ELHAM.** This isn't how people speak.

**MARJAN.** How do people speak to one another?

**ELHAM.** With words. That have meaning. Not like this. I don't know.

**MARJAN.** That's okay. Let's move on.

## Week 1: Friday

*(The class stands in a circle.* **MARJAN** *holds a large bouncy ball.)*

**MARJAN.**  Things that are green: Go!

*(She throws the ball to* **ELHAM**, *who will say her words then throw to* **GOLI**, *etc.)*

**ELHAM.**  Tree!

**GOLI.**  Apple!

**OMID.**  Leaves!

**GOLI.**  Baby banana!

**OMID.**  Pear!

**ELHAM.**  Ball for the tennis!

**ROYA.**  Apple!

**ELHAM.**  Apple was Goli get out of circle –

**MARJAN.**  Okay, it's only a game! But Roya, if you wouldn't mind stepping out. We're doing great! Goli, start us off: Items of clothing. Go.

**GOLI.**  Shirt!

**ELHAM.**  Pants!

**OMID.**  Blouse!

**ELHAM.**  Blue jean!

**GOLI.**  Shoe!

**ELHAM.**  Sock!

**GOLI.**  Jacket!

**OMID.**  Coat!

**ELHAM.**  Tie!

**OMID.** Windbreaker!

| **ELHAM.** | **GOLI.** |
|---|---|
| What? | Dress! |

**ELHAM.** Glove!

**OMID.** Collar!

**GOLI.** Glass! Is it glass?

**MARJAN.** So close, Goli! Did you mean glasses?

**GOLI.** Yes. Glasses.

**OMID.** Sorry, Goli.

**ELHAM.** Winderbreak what is winderbreak?

**OMID.** A windbreaker is a jacket.

**MARJAN.** Indeed, it is. Things you find in a classroom. Go!

**ELHAM.** Student!

**OMID.** A desk!

**ELHAM.** Chair!

**OMID.** An apple!

**ELHAM.** Pencil!

**OMID.** Uhuh syllabus!

**ELHAM.** Pen!

**OMID.** A ruler!

**ELHAM.** Textbook!

**OMID.** White-out!

**ELHAM.** Window! [**MARJAN.** *W*indow]

**OMID.** Scissors!

**ELHAM.** Wait wait wait come on –

**MARJAN.**  We have a winner!

(**GOLI** *and* **ROYA** *congratulate* **OMID**.)

**OMID.**  Sorry –

**ELHAM.**  Sorry, shouldn't you be in a more advanced class?

**OMID.**  This is the advanced class.

**ELHAM.**  Did you go to an American school?

**ROYA.**  There are no American schools anymore.

**ELHAM.**  Skill level needs to be dispersed evenly in a classroom. Or else it's – it's undispersed and we'll all fall behind –

**OMID.**  I have American cousins but my English sucks –

**ELHAM.**  No. **Windbreak?** That's not true.

**MARJAN.**  **You do speak quite well, Omid – I worry you'd become bored.**

**OMID.**  I have a green card interview in Dubai next month so –

**ROYA.**  They're harder on men. With visas and green cards. We all know that.

**GOLI.**  I've heard that, too.

**ROYA.**  Nader's took years. It nearly killed us.

**ELHAM.**  It may be marginally easier for the women but it's still extremely hard.

**OMID.**  I understand that. I've just. Respectfully, I have a right to think about my future, too.

**ELHAM.**  That's not what I said. I said you don't sound like you need any help. It was a compliment.

**MARJAN.**  **Alright! We've been speaking quite a lot of Farsi for one day.**

I suspect, Elham, that this may be a good range of skill.

Often, the more advanced speakers pull up the more challenged speakers.

This could be good for you. What do you think?

**ELHAM**.  Whatever you think is best.

## Week 1: Office Hours

(**ELHAM** *clutches her notebook as she talks to* **MARJAN**.)

(**MARJAN** *sets up the VCR.*)

**ELHAM.** I wanted to apologize for my behavior earlier. I'm not crazy.

**MARJAN. You're not the first competitive spirit to come through this classroom.**

**You're competitive. *Competitive.***

**ELHAM.** Oh. Right. I sort of lose my mind when I speak English. Not that I can speak English.

**MARJAN. You can speak English. Your written assignments are near perfect. And we'll loosen your tongue more. Your accent is quite strong.**

**ELHAM.** Yes, my accent is a war crime. Are you allowed to speak Farsi with me now? I won't tell anyone.

**MARJAN. Let's try it in English. Come on. Deep breath in. Deep breath out.**

**ELHAM.** Okay. Very good.

I eh. I take – I <u>taked</u> [**MARJAN.** took] *took* the TOEFL.

**MARJAN. You have taken the TOEFL before?**

**ELHAM.** I have *taken* the TOEFL five time.

**MARJAN. Five times?**

**ELHAM.** Five. Yes. Your ear is right.

**MARJAN. I had no idea. You didn't raise your hand when –**

**I should have been more discreet. It's, it's…**

**ELHAM.** Word is humiliation. I look it up.

**MARJAN.** That's a great word. And many students take the test more than once. It's very common.

**ELHAM.** I am – my school acceptance is not acceptance without good TOEFL.

**MARJAN.** I understand. I do. The stress.

(**OMID** *enters.*)

Just one moment, Omid.

**OMID.** Sorry, sorry.

(**OMID** *exits.*)

**ELHAM.** Please do not say to anyone about five time.

**MARJAN.** I would never.

**ELHAM.** This stuff doesn't come easy to me. Like it does for him.

**MARJAN.** Omid almost never speaks Farsi in class. It makes a difference. I know it's terrifying but you have to be brave. Be brave in English.

**ELHAM.** I'm sorry. I just wanted to tell you in my own words.

**MARJAN.** Would you like to stay and watch this with me? It's a romantic comedy. It would be wonderful training for your ear.

**ELHAM.** Oh. No. No thank you. I go another time. I have to go. I'm sorry.

**MARJAN.** It's alright.

**ELHAM.** Goodbye.

**MARJAN.** Bye.

(**OMID** *enters.*)

**OMID.**  Is now a good time?

**MARJAN.  How can I help you, Omid?**

**OMID.**  I'd like to reassure you: I will be a productive member of this class. I'll contribute.

**MARJAN.  I know you will.**

**OMID.**  I won't get bored.

**MARJAN.  English please.**

**OMID.  Sorry.**

**MARJAN.  Have you seen this film?**

**OMID.  Julia Roberts. My mom loves her.**

**MARJAN.  My daughter loves her, too. This copy is ancient.**

**OMID.  This woman has enormous teeth.**

**MARJAN.  I love her smile.**

**OMID.  No no I just mean you only find teeth like this in the west.**

**MARJAN.  That's true. They're – what's the word – strong.**

**OMID.  They're sturdy.**

**MARJAN.  They are!**

**OMID.  They could rip through wire. In a good way.**

**MARJAN.  That's right. That's it.**

**OMID.  This is British?**

**MARJAN.  Well, I lived in Manchester for nine years.**

**OMID.  You don't sound British.**

**MARJAN.  I was taught American English here.**

**OMID.  If you want a newer video, I can find a bootleg for you.**

MARJAN. Bootleg?

OMID. Bootleg, uh...it's a video – it's when they tape the movie in the theater –

MARJAN. Ohoh bootleg. I know bootleg.

OMID. I have a guy.

MARJAN. Do you?

OMID. Good quality. His camera never falls over.

MARJAN. The camera sometimes falls / over?

OMID. Yes but my guy stays steady, no heavy breathing. All of his are subtitled.

MARJAN. I don't want subtitles. I like to listen.

OMID. That makes sense.

    *(Beat.)*

You know, this is the most English I've spoken with anyone in a long time. And um. I made you laugh. In English. I didn't know I could do it. And I'm happy to be here speaking with you.

MARJAN. Likewise.

    *(Beat.)*

I've found it useful to show films during office hours. You're welcome to watch it with me. Sometimes understanding Hugh Grant takes two people.

OMID. Whenever you want.

MARJAN. Office hours will be fine.

    *(Beat.)*

OMID. Is that now?

MARJAN. Yes.

**OMID.**  I would love that.

    (**MARJAN** *plays the movie.*\* **OMID** *sits.*)

**MARJAN.**  Your English.

**OMID.**  I'm out of practice.

**MARJAN.**  No.

  No one speaks like you here.

---

\* A license to produce *English* does not include a performance license for any third-party or copyrighted video or film audio. Licensees should create an original video or secure permission to use a copyrighted video. For further information, please see Music and Third-Party Materials Use Note on page iii.

## Week 2: Monday

(**GOLI**, *at the front of the class, inserts a CD into the boombox.*)

**GOLI**. Hold on hold on let me... **Can I play it?**

**MARJAN**. **Whenever you're ready, darling.**

(**GOLI** *presses play. "She Bangs" by Ricky Martin plays at a high volume.*)

**ELHAM**. **Okay this is very loud.**

**GOLI**. **What?**

**ELHAM**. **I am deaf now.**

**ROYA**. **I am not.**

**MARJAN**. **Ladies, give Goli her room.**

**ELHAM**. **You give me injury to my head.**

**ROYA**. **You give me music to my head.**

**MARJAN**. **Goli, would you please turn it down?**

**GOLI**. Okay umsorry sorry. Here it is. Okay.

**I read now the words from Ricky Martin's song.**

(**GOLI** *reads half of the first verse of "She Bangs" aloud.*)

**I don't know.**

(*Beat.*)

**OMID**. **Screw everyone, Goli.**

**GOLI**. **Screw is what?**

**OMID**. **Just fuck everyone. Sorry, Marjan.**

**MARJAN**. **I think what Omid is telling you is speak, Goli. Please, continue.**

**GOLI.** Okay. I will fuck everyone.

> (**GOLI** *reads the second half of the first verse of*
> *"She Bangs" aloud.*)

**MARJAN.** I'm dying to hear your thoughts on these
words. Tell us.

**GOLI.** Yes, okay. Ricky Martin...is <u>on love</u> –

**MARJAN.** *In* love –

**GOLI.** In love in love.

Ricky Martin is in love with <u>woman</u> [**MARJAN.** a
woman] a woman who he thinks is born in May or
June.

But we do not know when she is born.

Or where she is from.

Maybe Iran! But probably not.

**MARJAN.** Maybe!

**GOLI.** This woman takes over the brain of Ricky Martin.

It is like when outside a car alarm is so loud for so
long but no one can find the car.

Or like when a bird flies into a window and the rest
of the day you can hear it.

**MARJAN.** Listen to yourself, Goli! You're a poet in
English.

> (**ELHAM** *raises her hand.*)

**GOLI.** Yes?

**ELHAM.** Do you want to speak English like Ricky
Martin speaks English?

**MARJAN.** Goli's room, Elham.

**ELHAM**.  But I can ask question about accent and speak
and have conversation. Yes no?

**MARJAN**.  With Goli's permission.

**GOLI**.  Okay.

**MARJAN**.  In English.

**ELHAM**.  Ricky Martin, <u>she</u> [**MARJAN**. he] does not
speak English-English.

**GOLI**.  Ricky Martin speaks very well good [**MARJAN**.
well] well –

**ELHAM**.  Omid speaks well and he does not sound
like Ricky Martin. Omid, does Ricky Martin have
accent?

**OMID**.  I guess.

**GOLI**.  And so what?

**ELHAM**.  All I'm saying though – **In your dream when
you speak English perfectperfect, who you are
sounding like?**

**GOLI**.  People like accent.

**ELHAM**.  They like English accent French accent not
your accent not my accent.

**GOLI**.  It is our bad English not our accent –

**ELHAM**.  **You tell me, Marjan, that we are improving
the accent** and the truth hurts but sorrysorry **Goli
people hear your accent and they go oh my god it is
so funny you are so stupid.**

**MARJAN**.  Elham –

**ELHAM**.  Okay if I have accent, bad TOEFL score. Omid
has accent, no green card. Roya's accent? Disaster.

**MARJAN**.  You've said your piece, Elham.

**ELHAM**.  **Okay I want to say one more one more one more I am helping you** okay you get it. You get it. Sorry.

(*Beat.*)

**MARJAN**.  **Would you mind bringing in something different next week? Perhaps an American song that you like?**

**GOLI**. **Yes I. Will. Do it.**

**MARJAN**. **You did a marvelous job today.**

**GOLI**. **Thank you.**

(*Beat.*)

I don't know. I like your accent.

## Week 2: Wednesday

(**ELHAM** *stands at the front, holding her notes.*)

**ELHAM**. Hello, I am Elham.

(*The class greets her.*)

Okay today for the show and the tell I am very much looking forward to sharing my research with you all.

**ROYA**. What is / research?

**ELHAM**. No questions I am speaking. Hold your – hold your horses. Yes?

**MARJAN**. Yes!

**GOLI**. Who holds horses?

**ROYA**. You do not hold horses for Goli / or me –

**ELHAM**. I hold them I am speaking –

**MARJAN**. (*Accent correction.*) Speaking.

**ELHAM**. Sorry speaking. Speaking.

(*Referring to notes again.*) According to scientists from the Royal Melbourne Institute of Technology in Melbourne Australia –

**MARJAN**. Elham darling, this is a speaking assignment.

**ELHAM**. I want to share with you all my medical school personal statement that I am accepted with.

**MARJAN**. I would love to hear that. Tell us.

**ELHAM**. It is a lot to memorize.

I do not know it.

**MARJAN**. You'll find it. I'm on the edge of the seat. According to scientists...

**ELHAM**. *(Folding notes in half.)* **According to scientists from the RMIT in Melbourne, Australia, many people suffer from gastrointestinal disorders. Fifteen per cent of people...will not get a proper diagnosis. So my research is...make less stomach pain for people.**

**MARJAN**. **To help people with stomach pain?**

**ELHAM**. **Yes I want to help to alleviate! To alleviate... pain. Because it is**

**debil – debril –**

**It is no use for suffering. Make less of suffering.**

> *(Beat.)*

**Okay I tell you this: my MCAT score is very very good. I get 40.**

**MARJAN**. **Your MCAT was conducted in English, no?**

**ELHAM**. **Yes.**

**MARJAN**. **Your English can't be so bad, then.**

**ELHAM**. **No MCAT is different.**

**I uh I study – I *will* study gastroenterology in Australia. I hope.**

**MARJAN**. **We have a future doctor among us!**

**ELHAM**. **One day.**

**MARJAN**. **And an Australian!**

**ELHAM**. **No but when I am passing TOEFL. Then yes I go.**

> *(Beat.)*

**And if I do very good – veryvery good I do teach aide.**

**MARJAN**. **Repeat that, please. That last part?**

**ELHAM.** Teach aide I am getting money for teach students in the university –

| **MARJAN.** | **OMID.** |
|---|---|
| Oh, a teaching – | Oh yeah a uh a a teaching assistant. |

**ELHAM.** Okay. Teaching assist.

**MARJAN.** Teaching assistant.

    *(Beat.)*

**ELHAM.** I bring in this because I don't know

Every day in here I feel like idiot

And I want everyone to know I am not idiot.

**MARJAN.** I am not *an idiot.*

**ELHAM.** I am not an idiot and also I am nice.

And also I am care-y. I care about the world andand...

I am nice.

**MARJAN.** English isn't your enemy.

**ELHAM.** It is feeling like yes.

**MARJAN.** English is not to be conquered. Embrace it.

You can be all the things you are in Farsi in English, too.

I always liked myself better in English.

**ELHAM.** Can we move it on? Please?

**MARJAN.** Sure.

## Week 2: Friday

*(The class listens to a recording of a conversation.)*

**MALE.** Hi, Jennifer.

**FEMALE.** Hey, Coach. I just thought I'd stop by to see what I missed while I was gone.

**MALE.** Well, I asked Sarah to go over our plan for the next game with you. We've been working real hard. She'll get you up to speed.

**FEMALE.** Great.

**MALE.** By the way, did you have a good time at your brother's wedding?

**FEMALE.** Oh, I had so much fun. The whole family was there! I saw cousins I hadn't seen in years.

**MALE.** I'm glad to hear that you enjoyed yourself.

**FEMALE.** I feel bad about missing basketball practice, though. I'm sorry about that.

**MALE.** Family is very important.

*(**MARJAN** pauses the recording.)*

**MARJAN.** What do we know?

We must know something! Anything at all. Roya, what do you know?

**ROYA.** I know nothing.

*(Beat.)*

**OMID.** She went to a wedding.

**MARJAN.** Yes! Whose wedding?

**GOLI.** Her cousin's wedding.

**ROYA.**  Her wedding.

**OMID.**  Her brother's. I think.

**MARJAN.**  Her brother's. And who is this man that she's speaking to right now? What is their relationship?

**ROYA.**  Brother.

**MARJAN.**  No.

**ROYA.**  But they go to wedding together.

**MARJAN.**  Well, she *went* to her brother's wedding but she's not speaking to her brother. So. Who is he?

**OMID.**  Her coach. Jennifer plays basketball.

**MARJAN.**  Mhm. And this wedding – how was it? Goli, what do we think?

**GOLI.**  I feel...she has good time at wedding.

**MARJAN.**  How so?

**GOLI.**  I feel in my heart her voice.

**OMID.**  She saw all her family. Her loved ones.

**MARJAN.**  Great. Let's continue.

> *(Unpause.)*

**MALE.**  One minute. There are a couple of other things I need to tell you.

**FEMALE.**  Oh, okay.

**MALE.**  First of all: I have good news. Everybody's getting a new team jacket.

**FEMALE.**  No way!

**MALE.**  A woman who played here twenty years ago saw one of our games. She wants to give back to the team.

**FEMALE.**  And she's paying for our new jackets?

**MALE.**  Yep.

**FEMALE.** How kind!

**MALE.** Isn't it great that former players still care so much about the program? Anyway, you need to fill out an order form. Bring it back as soon as possible so we can order. We could be wearing our jackets by our next game.

(*Pause.*)

**MARJAN.** How's Jennifer doing? Has she received good news? Bad news? Any ideas?

(*Beat.*)

Anyone? Goli... Roya... Elham?

**ELHAM.** (*Shaking head.*) No. No.

**MARJAN.** Omid?

**OMID.** Good news. A woman who a long time ago played on the basketball team wants to buy new jackets for the team. They're all really excited about it.

**ROYA.** How are you hearing / all that?

**ELHAM.** Have you heard this before or something?

**ROYA.** I have a headache.

**GOLI.** He has American family.

**ELHAM.** We all have American family. My American family voted for Bush. So.

**OMID.** Well. I watch BBC America.

**ELHAM.** I watch Al Jazeera America.

**OMID.** I listen to musicals.

**ELHAM.** I listen to Fergie.

I watch movie films.

*Indiana Jones*: American English.

*Muriel's Wedding*: Australian English.

*Love Actually*: **English English.**

**I listen and I listen and still it is like bees bzz bzz bzz**

My *head* how are you getting this?

**OMID.**  **I don't know. Maybe you don't want it.**

**ELHAM.**  Excuse me?

**OMID.**  **Maybe you don't want to / leave?**

**ELHAM.**  No one wants it more than me.

**MARJAN.**  **Elham –**

**ELHAM.**  Marjan, I'm sorry. I can't say it in English.

**OMID.**  **I don't know. They're not speaking that fast.**

**MARJAN.**  **You speak Farsi at this speed.**

**ROYA.**  They're speaking fast.

**GOLI.**  It's so fast.

## Week 2: Office Hours

(**MARJAN** *and* **OMID** *watch the credits roll.*)

(**MARJAN** *turns off the TV.*)

**MARJAN.** Good for them.

(*They laugh.*)

**OMID.** I wish I sounded like them. When I spoke English.

**MARJAN.** Like what?

**OMID.** Like easy.

**MARJAN.** You do.

I brought something.

(**MARJAN** *pulls out two cans of Coca-Cola.*\*)

(*Seeing his confusion.*) The lettering. In English. It's / American Coca-Cola –

**OMID.** Oh oh yes –

**MARJAN.** It's not exciting.

**OMID.** It is exciting.

**MARJAN.** A student found it for me. I miss seeing it. The English. I don't know. Would you like one?

**OMID.** I would love one.

(**MARJAN** *cleans the tops of the cans, opens them.*)

---

\* A license to produce *English* does not include a license to publicly display any branded logos or trademarked images. Licensees must acquire rights for any logos and/or images or create their own. For further information, please see Music and Third-Party Materials Use Note on page iii.

**MARJAN.** To your green card.

**OMID.** Thank you.

>*(They drink.)*

**MARJAN.** Alright.

>(**OMID** *and* **MARJAN** *re-arrange chairs.)*

**OMID.** Does your husband speak English?

**MARJAN.** No. He doesn't know it.

**OMID.** Is it enough for you –

to have halfway conversations with your students?

**MARJAN.** I love teaching English.

**OMID.** Must have been funny coming back.

To live in Farsi again.

**MARJAN.** Nine years isn't as long as you think.

**OMID.** Or you're the kind of person who could do anything.

**MARJAN.** I'm not.

**OMID.** I'm the kind of person who can barely do anything.

**MARJAN.** It took me two years alone to figure out the bus routes.

Which one of the lines went north/south, east/west.

And the sounds of the bus – the doors would *swoosh* open.

The buses here don't *swoosh*.

For nine years they called me Mary.

I liked Mary. For me.

**OMID.** Mary is a nice name.

**MARJAN.** When I came back here, I didn't know what to answer to.

**OMID.** Why did you come back?

**MARJAN.** We used to come back in those days.

**OMID.** I'm sorry. I'm being pushy.

**MARJAN.** You have questions. About your future. It's natural.

**OMID.** Can I ask you – can you really see me out there? In in America?

**MARJAN.** Yes. I can.

    *(Beat.)*

*(Re: the can.)* It's silly. To miss a thing like this.

**OMID.** I think I would miss it, too.

## Week 3: Monday

(**MARJAN** *stands at the front.*)

(*Written on the board:* NO CLASS WEDNESDAY.)

**MARJAN.** We're halfway through our course now, and I sense some frustration.

I understand how strange it feels to invite a foreign language into your body.

To reshape the workings of your tongue and your mouth but I wanted to talk to you today and ask you to try something.

If you are here to learn English,

I am going to ask you to agree that here

in this room

we are not Iranian.

We are not even on this continent.

Today I will ask you to feel any pull you have to your Iranian-ness and let it go.

Keep it outside the wall of this classroom.

(*Beat.*)

In this room, we are native speakers.

We think in English.

We laugh in English.

Our inhales, our exhales – we fill our lungs in English.

No more Farsi.

Can we agree to that? Yes? Thank you.

*(Beat.)*

**MARJAN.** For nine years, my name was Mary.

Marjan, it's – I love my name, but even a new name –

The smallest sacrifices can open our world.

**ELHAM.** Marjan is not hard to say.

**MARJAN.** The rewards are very huge –

**ELHAM.** Don't you think people can do us the courtesy of learning our names?

> *(**MARJAN** makes four columns on the chalkboard, labelled:)*
>
> *(*Elham, Goli, Roya, Omid.*)*
>
> *(She marks a tally in Elham's column.)*

**MARJAN.** Choose your Farsi wisely.

**ELHAM.** Your name is really pretty. If I had a girl, I / would –

> *(Another tally.)*

**MARJAN.** You have three more times to speak Farsi this week.

I'd like you to try this, Elham.

Every weird noise I teach you here today is for something much bigger than a test.

I'm here with you today because I want you to hear your voice and fall in love with what it becomes.

**ELHAM.** Our names they are our names. I am saying this correctly?

**MARJAN.** Yes.

**ROYA.** Marjan, can we take break?

**MARJAN.** Sure. I know that was a lot. Go go go.

*(Beat.)*

**ROYA.** I'm not sure, Marjan. Our mothers get to name us. Not foreigners.

## Week 3: Wednesday

*(**ELHAM** enters.)*

*(**ROYA** plays on her iPhone.)*

*(They are the only two in class.)*

**ELHAM.** Hi, Roya. How are you?

**ROYA.** I'm well. How are you?

**ELHAM.** Good.

Where the hell is everyone?

**ROYA.** People are rude.

**ELHAM.** I paid for three hours of class.

**ROYA.** You should demand a refund.

**ELHAM.** Is that an iPhone?

**ROYA.** Nader brought it for me from Canada. Look, you can touch the screen.

**ELHAM.** I know how an iPhone works.

**ROYA.** *(On the phone.)* **Nader hello there I am Roya again.**

**Red orange yellow green blue purple.**

**Yes okay thank you. Have a good one.**

I'm showing him I speak English.

**ELHAM.** Help me understand, Roya. You have the PR card. That's half the battle. Learn English when you get there, the old-fashioned way.

**ROYA.** They speak English in the house so.

**ELHAM.** They should be begging you to teach her Farsi.

**ROYA.** They want her to grow up in English.

It's my fault. I've been promising to learn it since she was born.

He's getting prickly about it. It's fine.

*(On the phone.)* Why isn't it ringing I don't hear a ring –

**Nader hello there I am Roya.**

**I am here to tell you numbers. I know all the numbers now.**

**Forty-three. Five hundred and thirty-eight.**

**And.**

**Seven.**

**Have a good one.**

How was that?

**ELHAM.** Great numbers.

**ROYA.** I just. Want her to know me.

**ELHAM.** You're her grandma.

**ROYA.** So?

**ELHAM.** So that little girl will be immediately in love with you.

**ROYA.** Nader put her on the phone with me the other day. I can't even say her name right.

**ELHAM.** Let me be real with you... **Claire** is a weird name.

**ROYA.** I begged them to name her something even remotely Iranian.

**ELHAM.** Sure. Yeah.

**ROYA.** But he wants her to be Canadian and I want to be her grandmother.

**ELHAM.** You call him a lot, don't you?

**ROYA.** I won't apologize for my displays of affection, however vigorous.

**ELHAM.** No, I know. Of course not.

*(Beat.)*

Is it going straight to voicemail?

**ROYA.** Yes. Why?

**ELHAM.** No reason.

*(Beat.)*

Roya, do you like me?

**ROYA.** Do I like you? You're a little sensitive in Farsi, aren't you? Who knew?

**ELHAM.** I think he's ignoring your calls. That's what happens. When it goes straight to voicemail.

*(Beat.)*

**ROYA.** No, he's not.

**ELHAM.** That's not to say he couldn't be at work –

**ROYA.** That's a terrible thing to say.

**ELHAM.** I would never ignore my mother's calls.

**ROYA.** You're very smart, Elham.

But you're very rude.

In Farsi, you balance yourself out.

But wherever you land, you're going to have quite a hard time adjusting.

Because in English, you won't have redeeming qualities.

I take no pleasure in saying that. Really.

*(Beat.)*

**ELHAM.**  I don't think anyone's coming.

Bye.

**ROYA.**  Bye.

     (**ELHAM** *leaves.*)

*(On the phone.)* **Nader hello I am Roya again. Please call me. Thank you.**

## Week 3: Friday

*(The class stands in a circle.)*

**MARJAN.** Wa!

**ALL.** Wa!

**MARJAN.** Your lips are small, tight. In a circle. Wa!

**ALL.** Wa!

**MARJAN.** Wow!

**ALL.** Wow!

**MARJAN.** Lips out, Roya. Weird weird weird!

**ALL.** Weird weird weird!

**MARJAN.** Welcome, Wendy!

**ALL.** Welcome, Wendy!

**MARJAN.** *(Again.)* I hear a v. Welcome, Wendy!

**ALL.** Welcome, Wendy!

**MARJAN.** When we were weeping!

**ALL.** When we were weeping!

**MARJAN.** Wicked Witch of the West!

**ALL.** Wicked Witch of the West!

**MARJAN.** Elham.

**ELHAM.** I know sorrysorry.

**MARJAN.** The veels – the wheels on the bus!

**ALL.** The wheels on the bus!

## Week 3: Office Hours

(**MARJAN** *and* **OMID** *watch a movie.*\*)

**MARJAN.** Did you hear me slip today?

**OMID.** Slip? How?

**MARJAN.** Did you hear me... [can't find a better word]

**OMID.** I don't know what / you mean –

**MARJAN.** I uh. I heard my accent today. So loud. My ears are still... [ringing]

**OMID.** You made a mistake.

**MARJAN.** So you did hear.

It's funny what the years do. I used to trick natives.

**OMID.** I really – barely heard it.

(*Beat.*)

Wa. Water.

(*Beat.*)

The wheels on the bus.

**MARJAN.** The wheels on the bus.

**OMID.** Willy Wonka.

**MARJAN.** Willy Wonka.

**OMID.** It's a movie.

**MARJAN.** Yes I know.

---

\* A license to produce *English* does not include a performance license for any third-party or copyrighted video or film audio. Licensees should create an original video or secure permission to use a copyrighted video. For further information, please see Music and Third-Party Materials Use Note on page iii.

**OMID.**  We should watch it.

**MARJAN.**  We should. *We*. Should.

**OMID.**  See. You're perfect.

**MARJAN.**  When is your birthday?

**OMID.**  February. When is yours –

**MARJAN.**  Summer. Nevermind. I thought we might –
we don't.

> *(Beat.)*

It's nice, isn't it. Like we're somewhere else.

**OMID.**  Almost.

> *(Beat.)*

**MARJAN.**  Thank you.

## Week 4: Monday

(**ROYA**, *alone in the room, speaks into her iPhone. [Note: Nader's English is noticeably accented.]*)

**IPHONE.** Hello there. You have reached Nate Abedi. Please leave your contact information and I will get back to you as soon as possible. Have a good one!

**ROYA.** Hello sweetie pie. I am Maman. Roya Abedi. Where are you?

Tell me.

Okay.

*(She hangs up. Calls again.)*

**IPHONE.** Hello there. You have reached Nate Abedi. Please leave your contact information and I will get back to you as soon as possible. Have a good one!

**ROYA.** Hello there. You have reached Nate Abedi. Please leave your contact information and I will get back to you as soon as possible. Have a good one!

I think Nader is not so hard name to say for Canadians.

Nate is sound dog the makes.

Claire is...

Why you give my granddaughter name I cannot say?

Families aren't meant to live this way.

Call me. I need to buy my ticket.

I am sorry to speak Farsi.

*(Beat.)*

**ROYA.**  I hope you not forget.

Nate is not your name.

## Week 4: Wednesday

(**ROYA** *stands at the front of the class with a piece of paper.*)

**MARJAN**. Whenever you're ready, Roya.

**ROYA**. First I tell you words of voicemail from Nader in English.

I write down words [**MARJAN**. the words]. The words says [**MARJAN**. say] say: Mom. You call me now. We need to talk. About when you are coming to visit. With us. Don't buy your ticket yet.

(*Beat.*)

His English is good but I have questions.

Number 1: who is *Mom*? I am not *mom* I am *maman*.

Number 2: The word *visit* is not the word *live*. Visit is come for one week, two week.

Uh... I uh... I forgot. There is more voicemail but his English is fast.

**OMID**. Do you want help?

**ROYA**. No thank you sweetie pie.

But now but *now* he leave me voicemail in Farsi. The words say:

I just want to talk to you. Are you okay? Is everything okay? We should talk about – I'm up to my ears in work and...call me, okay? I'll talk to you soon. Bye.

(*Beat.*)

Do you hear

how much more

soft

**ROYA.** he is

　　in his mother tongue?

　　Do you hear

　　he remembers where he is from

　　and who he comes from?

　　He forget in English

　　but in Farsi

　　he remember.

　　Now you will listen:

　　　　(**ROYA** *inserts a CD into the boombox. She finds the track. Presses play. An old-school Iranian song plays.*\*)

**MARJAN.** Roya, is this the correct song?

**ROYA.** What is wrong?

**MARJAN.** This isn't in English.

**ROYA.** You talk about Farsi like it's a stench after a long day's work. Tell me, Marjan, what is it about where we're from that you find so repulsive?

**MARJAN.** I know you're upset.

**ROYA.** We should remember that we come from this.

And our voluntary migration from this is something we should be grieving.

This is my song. I would be ever so grateful for your attention.

---

\* A license to produce *English* does not include a performance license for any third-party or copyrighted music other than "She Bangs." Licensees should create an original composition or use music in the public domain. For further information, please see the Music and Third-Party Materials Use Note on page iii.

*(The class relents. The song is unapologetically Iranian.)*

**(MARJAN** *tallies* **ROYA.***)*

## Week 4: Friday

*(The class stands in a circle with the bouncy ball.)*

*(Note: **ROYA** is absent and does not make any further appearances.)*

**MARJAN.** Things you find in a kitchen. Go!

**ELHAM.** Fork!

**OMID.** Dish!

**MARJAN.** Plate!

**GOLI.** Napkin?

**OMID.** Spoon!

**MARJAN.** Stove!

**ELHAM.** Chair! Kitchen / chair!

**GOLI.** Sink!

**OMID.** Placemat!

**MARJAN.** Faucet!

**GOLI.** Nono no no I don't / know

**MARJAN.** You can do this, Goli!

**ELHAM.** I am sorry Goli but it is time you leave circle have a good day!

**OMID.** Next time, Goli –

**MARJAN.** Keep going!

**ELHAM.** Knife!

**OMID.** Spatula!

**ELHAM.** Pot!

**MARJAN.** Pan!

**ELHAM**. Oven!

**MARJAN**. Potholder!

**OMID**. Bowl!

**MARJAN**. Coffeemaker!

**ELHAM**. Sponge!

**MARJAN**. Sheef!

**OMID**. Apron!

**ELHAM**. What is sheef?

**MARJAN**. Chef thethe cook

**ELHAM**. I don't know what is the sheef whatever you say –

**MARJAN**. I meant chef –

**ELHAM**. You say sheef –

**OMID**. Cut it out –

**ELHAM**. He says sheef –

**OMID**. She said.

**ELHAM**. Okay yes she said sheef.

**MARJAN**. It's really no problem! Even the teachers make mistakes.

**ELHAM**. I have no mistake yet so Omid and I play.

**OMID**. Measuring cups!

**ELHAM**. Refrigerator!

**OMID**. Towel!

**ELHAM**. Table!

**OMID**. Whisk!

**ELHAM**. Cabinet!

**OMID**. Cookbook!

**ELHAM.**  Microwave!

**OMID.**  Dish soap!

**ELHAM.**  Dish washer!

**OMID.**  Spices!

**ELHAM.**  Garbage can!

**OMID.**  Blender!

**ELHAM.**  Jar!

**OMID.**  Tupperware!

**ELHAM.**  Toaster!

**OMID.**  Uh uh uh oh god um –

**MARJAN.**  Three, two –

**ELHAM.**  Mop for if you spill unfortunately Omid you
are loser –

**MARJAN.**  Good job, Elham!

**ELHAM.**  I fucking win –

**MARJAN.**  Celebrate in English, please –

**ELHAM.**  I am sorry. Sorry.

**MARJAN.**  Job well done. Keep this up and this will be
your last TOEFL.

*(Beat.)*

**GOLI.**  You have taken the TOEFL before?

**ELHAM.**  Many of the people take test twice.

**GOLI.**  Oh / yeah –

**OMID.**  You've taken it twice?

**ELHAM.**  I have taken it a little times.

**OMID.**  A few times?

**ELHAM.**  Don't correct me.

**OMID.**  Just trying to help.

**ELHAM.**  Are you going to mark him, Marjan? He's speaking Farsi. Or is it just me who can't speak Farsi in here.

(**MARJAN** *tallies* **OMID** *and* **ELHAM.**)

**GOLI.**  The test is hard, Elham –

**ELHAM.**  Yeah I know that.

## Week 4: Office Hours

(**ELHAM** *and* **GOLI** *sit.*)

(*A backpack sits in the corner.*)

**GOLI.** I wonder where Marjan is –

**ELHAM.** Oh god, Goli. Please don't.

**GOLI.** We can be practicing English.

**ELHAM.** No. No English or I'll throw you out the window.

**GOLI.** Okay. Sorry.

She's here somewhere. That's Omid's backpack.

**ELHAM.** God she is so in *love* with him.

**GOLI.** Really?

**ELHAM.** Yes hello she has the most obvious boner for him.

**GOLI.** (*Nervous giggle.*) Boner.

**ELHAM.** You know, you deserve as much time as any other student. Don't be so nice.

**GOLI.** I like being nice.

**ELHAM.** Where are you going next year? Are you leaving or.

**GOLI.** I'm not sure yet.

The TOEFL score is valid for two years.

So we'll see.

**ELHAM.** What's your question? I've probably asked it.

**GOLI.** I guess I don't have like a specific question. I sort of just wanted to speak with her? Like have a conversation or something?

(*Beat.*)

**ELHAM.** I have this amazing dream sometimes that the Persian Empire kept growing.

And Cyrus the Great would still be our king.

Instead of the Americans, the British, everyone

telling us what to speak and how to say it, all of us would speak Farsi.

**GOLI.** Well, I like English.

**ELHAM.** Why's that?

**GOLI.** You know like, no one really listens to me in Farsi but

I don't know when I speak English it's like

there are no question marks at the end of my sentences and I'm

three or four inches taller?

**ELHAM.** You're eighteen, Goli. That's how eighteen feels.

**GOLI.** I guess.

>*(Beat.)*

My mom is outside. I hope you have a nice weekend.

**ELHAM.** You too.

>*(**ELHAM** erases her tallies on the board, adds to Omid's.)*

>*(She starts to doodle. **MARJAN** enters, a little startled.)*

Sorry I didn't mean to –

**MARJAN. Can you erase that?** *(Motions erase.)* **Erase.**

>*(**ELHAM** erases.)*

**Do you have a question?**

**ELHAM.** Um.

    *(Beat.)*

Why don't you like me?

**MARJAN. I'm sorry?**

**I like you.**

**ELHAM.** I work really hard.

    *(Beat.)*

**MARJAN. Why aren't you practicing English with me right now?**

**ELHAM.** I need to really speak with you.

I'm not sleeping.

I need at least a 94 and I'm like, really freaking out.

**MARJAN. You did well today. You won against Omid!**

**ELHAM.** It took everything in me.

**MARJAN. You're learning a new language, Elham. It takes so much dedication –**

**ELHAM.** I'm depleted. This is coming from a person who's taken the MCAT.

**MARJAN. You hate this language.**

**You put in such a fight.**

**Do you think you can learn a language that way?**

**ELHAM.** But you're not – Marjan, I need help.

**MARJAN. I understand. You're terrified.**

**And I am helping you by speaking English with you.**

    *(Beat.)*

**Today was – it was an honest mistake. I slipped.**

**ELHAM.** I guess it's probably better. That everyone knows.

**MARJAN. I'm so sorry that happened.**

**ELHAM.** Are you? Because you just stood there when –

**MARJAN. I'm so sorry.**

**ELHAM.** You can apologize to me in Farsi.

And we'll be cool.

**MARJAN. Elham. I feel – I really –**

**ELHAM.** I am asking for two words. Please.

**MARJAN. Why?**

**ELHAM.** Because I want to hear *you* tell me.

**MARJAN. I really am sorry, Elham.**

> (**ELHAM** *exits.*)

> (**MARJAN** *erases the whiteboard.*)

> (**OMID** *enters.*)

**OMID. What are we watching today?**

**MARJAN. Today – what if we spoke to one another today?**

**OMID. Spoke. Like –**

**MARJAN. Like talk.**

**OMID.** It'd be a pleasure. To talk to you.

**MARJAN. In English, still.**

**OMID. Any language. I don't care.**

**How are you?**

**MARJAN. I am good. How are you?**

**OMID. Great. I'm great.**

**OMID.** What's your favorite color?

**MARJAN.** Yellow. A dark yellow. Is there a name for it –

**OMID.** Mustard. Mustard?

**MARJAN.** Mustard, yes.

**OMID.** Do you know. I could do this all day. With you.

What will um. What will you be doing this weekend?

**MARJAN.** My daughter downloaded a film for me.

*Love Actually.* Have you seen it?

**OMID.** No.

**MARJAN.** I have tried to watch but I am having trouble.
They speak faster than I remember.

**OMID.** I don't think they even understand eachother.

(*Beat.*)

**MARJAN.** I wonder if you think I am funny.

**OMID.** What do you mean?

**MARJAN.** Am I a joke?

**OMID.** What?

**MARJAN.** Maybe it is ridiculous what I do.

My English, my Farsi – these two languages, they
[war] in my head.

And the Farsi is winning.

Do you know sometimes I think you can only speak
one language?

You can know two but –

I'm sorry.

**OMID.** Don't be sorry.

**MARJAN.** I feel like I'm disappearing.

*(Beat.)*

**OMID**. Did your visa not get renewed? Is that why you came back?

**MARJAN**. It wasn't my visa.

I can't quite remember.

I wish I could tell you.

**OMID**. I think you made the right decision.

**MARJAN**. I guess I belong here.

**OMID**. Is it a terrible thing? To belong here?

It's sort of a miracle, isn't it. To belong anywhere.

**MARJAN**. Your future is in English.

You do not belong here.

I like that about you.

**OMID**. Do you ever think about who you would be

if you never had to think about staying or leaving?

*(Beat.)*

**MARJAN**. If I had stayed. I think. I have this feeling. My hair would be longer. And my feet would ache less. But.

**OMID**. You don't know that. You don't.

*(Beat.)*

**MARJAN**. When I speak English. My ears ring.

But your English. Floats along the water.

One day you will be far away from here.

I wonder who I will speak with then.

## Week 5: Monday

>   (**GOLI** *and* **OMID** *stand at the front of the
>   class.*)

**OMID.**  Ready, pal?

**GOLI.**  Ready, pal. Marjan, we are ready to have a
conversation.

**ELHAM.**  Is Roya / coming?

**MARJAN.**  Let's go ahead.

**ELHAM.**  Did she drop or –

**MARJAN.**  Roya is fine. Whenever you two are ready.

>   (*Beat.*)

**GOLI.**  Hi, Omid.

**OMID.**  Hi, Goli.

**GOLI.**  I am very happy we are having a conversation
today.

**OMID.**  Me, too.

**GOLI.**  How did you sleep last night?

**OMID.**  I slept very well! I slept for eight hours. How
long did you sleep last night?

**GOLI.**  I slept for nine hours. Nine is good for me. Ten is
good for me. So is eleven, twelve –

**OMID.**  Are you a good sleeper?

**GOLI.**  Yes. And I want to say to you: Congratulations!

**OMID.**  Oh – why –

**GOLI.**  On on on what is word for will be married but no
marriage yet?

*(Beat.)*

**MARJAN.** Engaged.

**GOLI.** Congratulations, Omid!

**MARJAN.**                              **ELHAM.**
   Congratulations!            Congratulations.

**MARJAN.** When did this –

**OMID.** Saturday.

*(Beat.)*

**MARJAN.** Go ahead. You're doing great.

**GOLI.** We have mutual person on Facebook so I see!

**OMID.** Yeah.

**GOLI.** Yes. So. How are you today?

**OMID.** I'm good. How are you?

**GOLI.** I am very good.

**OMID.** Good.

**GOLI.** Me, too. I have never been better.

**MARJAN.** Goli, your English is getting so good.

**GOLI.** Thank you.

*(Beat.)*

   Omid, do you want to ask me a question?

**OMID.** Yeah. Sure. Uh. Let me uh...

*(Beat.)*

**GOLI.** Okay I can ask. Where uh. Where. Do...
   I cannot think of one question.
   Sorry.

**ELHAM.** Congratulations, big guy! May you live a thousand years of prosperity!

**OMID. Thanks.**

**MARJAN. Elham.**

**ELHAM.** I'll take the tally. This is a momentous occasion and I can't wish him well in English.

> *(Tally 1.)*

If I may – and I will:

> *(Tally 2.)*

I am a sensational wedding guest. You would not regret inviting me.

**MARJAN. That's three.**

> *(Tally 3.)*

**ELHAM.** I don't know how to say it in English –

> *(Tally 4.)*

**MARJAN. Four.**

> (**MARJAN** *holds up the marker as a final warning.*)

**ELHAM. I am sorry.**

> (**MARJAN** *closes the cap.*)

## Week 5: Wednesday

(**ELHAM**, **GOLI**, *and* **OMID** *take a practice test.*)

(**OMID**'s *leg fidgets.*)

**ELHAM**. Can you not?

(*His leg stops moving.*)

Goli, you are where?

**GOLI**. I am on seven.

What section you are on?

**ELHAM**. Three.

(*Beat.*)

Marjan can we pause timer please?

**MARJAN**. We'll go through all the questions at the end. I promise.

**ELHAM**. Okay.

(**ELHAM** *returns her attention to the test.*)

(*But* **OMID**'s *page-turning is distracting.*)

You are done?

**OMID**. Don't worry about it, Borat.

(*Beat.*)

**ELHAM**. What did you say to me?

**OMID**. Sorry sorry. It was a joke.

(**ELHAM** *returns her attention to her test.*)

(*But she can't shake it off.*)

**ELHAM**. No.

**MARJAN.** Try to push it through.

**ELHAM.** Are you hearing what he says?

**MARJAN.** Pardon me?

**ELHAM.** He says – he says –

**GOLI.** He called her –

**OMID.** I'm sorry.

**ELHAM.** How I learn when I I I I –

**MARJAN.** What?

**ELHAM.** You do not want being my teacher okay okay but then you have you are Goli's teacher be Goli's teacher –

**MARJAN.** I cannot understand what you / are saying.

**ELHAM.** Yes you are understand me stop just stop I know you know what I'm saying –

**GOLI.** I do not think you hear what we heard –

**OMID.** I'm sorry –

**MARJAN.** What happened?

**ELHAM.** He he he talks about my accent –

**MARJAN.** Well your accent is strong and you're talking through the practice test, Elham –

**ELHAM.** Do you think you could just for one fucking second stop playing favorites –

  *(Fifth tally for* **ELHAM.***)*

**MARJAN.** That's five. Pack up.

 Do you understand me?

**ELHAM.** Vhat?

**MARJAN.** *W*hat. *W*hat. Your accent is giving me a headache.

*(Beat.)*

**ELHAM.**  There are two hours of class left.

**MARJAN.**  **We'll see you next class.**

    *(**ELHAM** exits.)*

## Week 5: Office Hours

(**OMID** *stands before* **MARJAN** *with a miniature toy bus.*)

**OMID.** Last weekend, I was in Tehran.

And I found it. They sell these near the –

**MARJAN.** I should be giving you a gift.

**OMID.** No –

**MARJAN.** Congratulations.

**OMID.** Thank you.

**MARJAN.** You must be so happy.

**OMID.** I am.

**MARJAN.** It's very exciting.

**OMID.** It was – I mean –

It all happened quickly. In a good way.

**MARJAN.** Of course.

(*Beat.*)

You know for your green card, you will have to apply as a married couple. It makes your chances – makes the chances –

**OMID.** Lessens the chances.

**MARJAN.** Lessens the chances. Thank you.

**OMID.** We're not going.

**MARJAN.** You should at least keep your appointment.

**OMID.** I can leave. When I want. I have a passport.

An American passport.

*(Beat.)*

**MARJAN.** **When did you – when did you become a citizen?**

**OMID.** **I guess when I was born there.**

*(Beat.)*

**We're staying here.**

**We don't want to leave.**

*(Beat.)*

**MARJAN.** Okay. That's your decision to make.

**OMID.** You're speaking Farsi with me now.

That's fine. I don't care.

You only like me in English but I like you in both languages.

**MARJAN.** Why would you take this class?

**OMID.** I don't – I don't really uh –

**MARJAN.** You speak English. You have a passport.

And you're just – it's nothing to you?

**OMID.** I don't want it.

**MARJAN.** That is so immensely wasteful.

*(Beat.)*

**OMID.** Maybe you. Regret coming back –

**MARJAN.** I don't.

**OMID.** But I don't really. Want to. Anymore.

I kind of just want to be here. When my family came back –

**MARJAN.** I didn't say I regretted it –

**OMID**. Why do you only like me in English?

Why do you only – like everything in English?

**MARJAN**. I don't. I mean – I don't.

**OMID**. I don't think. I want to live like that.

**MARJAN**. Then why are you staying?

**OMID**. Because we came back. Our English isn't –

You don't remember? What it's like. To have an accent.

**MARJAN**. You barely have an accent.

**OMID**. I thought you would get it. I thought – Who else knows what we know.

**MARJAN**. Well, you and I are different. You're a citizen.

*(Beat.)*

**OMID**. You know, speaking to you. In Farsi. It's different.

Like it's actually the first real conversation we've had.

And I. I finally feel peace, Marjan. I finally feel –

*(Beat.)*

Please don't tell anyone.

**MARJAN**. I think your classmates deserve to know. But I won't.

*(**OMID** finally hands her the bus.)*

**OMID**. I thought it might look like the one you took in Manchester but how would I know.

**MARJAN**. Mine was green.

*(Beat.)*

**OMID**. There's so much happiness here.

I really / believe that.

**MARJAN.** I live very well.

I do.

## Week 6: Monday

(**OMID** *stands at the front with an American passport in his hand.*)

**OMID**. **Hello, Class.**

**I'm Omid.**

**And this is my American passport.**

(*Beat.*)

**GOLI**. **You said –**

**OMID**. **I know.**

NoIknow.

I'd like to just do this in Farsi and I know – if you don't –

(*Beat.*)

**GOLI**. Can I see that?

**OMID**. Yeah here it is.

(*Beat.*)

So I guess I should tell you:

My father became a citizen in 1980. My mother in 1982.

I'm the youngest of four.

All of us born in the great state of Ohio.

And we'd go back and forth between here and there but

we moved back here for good when I was about thirteen.

And I guess some part of me always thought we would go back but.

**GOLI**. You're American.

**OMID**. I'm a dual citizen.

**GOLI.** You were born in the United States.

**OMID.** I've lived most of my life here.

**ELHAM. You are a native speaker.**

(*Beat.*)

**OMID.** I'm so sorry, Elham –

**GOLI.** You speak perfect English. You speak better than Marjan. Sorry, Marjan.

**OMID.** I know what perfect English sounds like and I do not speak perfect English.

(*Beat.*)

**GOLI. I think you come here to –**

**Wow, yes, it is so funny that we cannot pronounce the words you can.**

**It is so funny when are when we do not know the right word.**

**OMID.** That was never my intention. Ever.

**GOLI. When you say you do not speak English perfect you know it is not a fact.**

**OMID.** I know that's what you think.

But the only place I speak perfect English is here.

I think I used to speak perfect English –

But now –

My English is – you can hear the gap between not from here, not from there.

I think I live there: in that gap.

But in here, I was from somewhere.

Or I was from nowhere.

**OMID.** I didn't have an accent.

I was...one...thing?

All my life, I've felt like half a thing?

Maybe you don't –

You know, I envy you.

That you've always been from here.

You know what you are.

Anyway.

Does that make sense or –

*(Beat.)*

**ELHAM. It says it is expire.**

**Two years ago.**

**You do not use it?**

**OMID. I visited from time to time.**

**ELHAM. You do not think...it is feeling like** [a waste]...

**OMID.** If I could give it to you –

**ELHAM.** You wouldn't.

*(Beat.)*

**MARJAN. Unfortunately, this course is designed for advanced learners not native speakers. Please call the student office. They will be able to issue a refund for the remaining sessions.**

**OMID. I'm sorry.**

**MARJAN. Let's move on.**

## Week 6: Wednesday

*(The class, now only* **MARJAN, ELHAM,** *and* **GOLI,** *move in a circle.)*

**MARJAN.** Wow!

**ALL.** Wow!

**MARJAN.** White!

**ALL.** White!

**MARJAN.** Elham, lips. Welcome, Wendy!

**ALL.** Welcome, Wendy!

**MARJAN.** *(Re: lips.)* Small and tight. Winter wedding!

**ALL.** Winter wedding!

**MARJAN.** Warm warm water!

**ALL.** Warm warm water!

**MARJAN.** When we were weeping!

**ALL.** When we were weeping!

**MARJAN.** Elham.

**ELHAM.** Yes?

**MARJAN.** Did you hear that?

That was good.

**ELHAM.** Thank you.

**MARJAN.** That's great.

**ELHAM.** Okay.

## Week 6: Friday

> (**MARJAN** *stands at the front of the class,*
> *which now consists of only* **GOLI**.)

**MARJAN.** I was going to present my show and tell today
but it seems a little silly to present to just you.

**GOLI.** I want to hear your show and tell.

**MARJAN.** You do?

Are you –

Alright.

Hello, Goli.

**GOLI.** Hello, Marjan.

**MARJAN.** My name is Marjan. As you know. This is my
bus.

> (*She shows her miniature toy bus.*)

Every day for nine years, I took the bus.

It looked a little like this.

*The wheels in a bus they around and around.*

There's a children's song –

**GOLI.** Is it about a bus?

**MARJAN.** It's about school. Or it's.

*The wheels on a bus they go around and around*

*The wheels on a bus it goes around*

*The wheels on*

> (*Beat.*)

I grew up in Karaj. Never really took the bus there.

**GOLI.** Whoa.

**MARJAN.** It's our last day together. Might as well break the rule.

**GOLI.** You sound so like. I don't know!

**MARJAN.** I must sound so strange to you in Farsi.

**GOLI.** Um. Yeah a little. Yeah.

**MARJAN.** One morning after I'd been living in Manchester for maybe – god, I can't remember how long I'd been there – but I took the bus. A woman asked me for directions to the city center and I gave them to her. She just thought I...belonged there and...

>   *(Beat.)*

When you speak another language – a language that's not yours it's –

My god, you just feel so loud all the time. Like all the worst parts of your voice are being filtered through a microphone.

Your head hurts and the days feel longer.

You go years without making anyone laugh.

No one has any idea that you were the top of your class.

Or that you're adventurous or optimistic or that you're kind. Really kind.

*You* start to forget that you're adventurous and optimistic and kind.

How long can you live in isolation from yourself?

You need to ask yourself that.

But if you can hold on...it's um...

It's everything.

**MARJAN.** Because one day, the voice that comes out of your mouth is one that you love.

It's something I can't quite…

**GOLI.** That sounds amazing.

**MARJAN.** Well, it's such a pretty day.

Get some rest. Take a walk. Don't study the day before the test.

I think that's about everything that I can impart to you.

Actually, I should ask: Do you have any questions?

**GOLI.** Um. Does your family speak English?

**MARJAN.** No, no. Well, my daughter has picked up bits and pieces over the years. From me. From movies. You know.

**GOLI.** Why'd you come back?

**MARJAN.** Why'd I come back?

*(Beat.)*

I got tired.

**GOLI.** Are you tired now?

**MARJAN.** You know, I don't – I don't know.

*(Beat.)*

**GOLI.** Thank you, Marjan. For everything.

**MARJAN. I wish you the best of luck on your exam.**

## Epilogue

*(One month later.)*

*(The classroom is empty except for* **ELHAM**, *who is doodling on the whiteboard.)*

*(***MARJAN*** enters.)*

**MARJAN.** Elham?

**ELHAM.** Oh, sorry –

**MARJAN.** Sorry, I didn't mean to scare you – your classroom will be across the hall. You're – I'm a little envious. That room doesn't heat up like an oven like this one does.

**ELHAM.** You should make a little noise.

*(***ELHAM*** starts erasing.)*

**MARJAN.** You don't have to do that.

I'm sure you noticed but I won't be your instructor.

**ELHAM.** What are you teaching?

**MARJAN.** Introductory.

**ELHAM.** Beginners.

**MARJAN.** No TOEFL. No exams. No frantic graduate students. Can you imagine?

Eleven, twelve-year-olds. It's not a bad age. Mushier minds. Makes my job easier.

**ELHAM.** Did your students not perform well on the test?

**MARJAN.** The test is more rigorous some years.

**ELHAM.** The reading comp was brutal.

**MARJAN.** I heard.

**ELHAM.** Words that looked made up.

**MARJAN**.  I'm sorry. Really.

**ELHAM**.  You'll probably have to speak Farsi with the beginners.

(*Beat.*)

**MARJAN**.  Listen, I – if you want to go down the private tutoring road, I can recommend some really wonderful teachers. I'd be more than happy to connect you. Just let me know.

**ELHAM**.  **I scored 99.**

**I pass.**

**More than pass.**

**MARJAN**.  Elham, that's an excellent score!

**ELHAM**.  **I qualify to teaching assist now.**

**MARJAN**.  What amazing news.

**ELHAM**.  **I am more than proficient. I am it says superior.**

**I can speak English very well. That is what the TOEFL says to me.**

**MARJAN**.  Yes, yes that's – I'm so happy for you –

**ELHAM**.  **You should speak English with me, Marjan. I speak English very well.**

**MARJAN**.  You don't need to prove anything to me.

**ELHAM**.  **I would like to speak English. If you please.**

(*Beat.*)

**MARJAN**.  **As you wish.**

**ELHAM**.  **Thank you.**

**MARJAN**.  **It is my pleasure.**

**ELHAM**.  **No one hates this language more than I hate.**

MARJAN.  I sensed that very early.

ELHAM.  I like my native tongue.

MARJAN.  Of course –

ELHAM.  No, I like Elham when she speaks Farsi.

(Beat.)

You are Iranian but your English is a lot of things.

It wants to be American and some of the time British and now it does not know what it is.

When I speak English, I know

I will always be

stranger.

Okay I know what I sound like. I hear my voice too.

But I am hearing myself.

I hear myself very loud.

I am hearing my sister and traffic in the morning and my chemistry teacher from in the high school.

I hear my home.

What do you hear?

(The next section is heard in real Farsi.)

MARJAN.  Man – manam hamina ro mishnavam vali... nemidunam.

[I – I hear it too but... I don't know.]

ELHAM.  Bikhial.

[Nevermind.]

MARJAN.  Javabam hamoon bood.

[That was my answer.]

**ELHAM.**  Bashe.

[Okay.]

(*Beat.*)

**MARJAN.**  Shayatam ye rooz lahjeye khodet ba gozashte zaman avaz she.

[And maybe one day your accent will change with time.]

**ELHAM.**  Momken ham hast nashe –

[Or not –]

**MARJAN.**  Ye roozam to paye telephone yoho mishnavi ke lahjat khareji-eh. Momkene oon rooz ham berese.

[And one day on the phone you'll suddenly hear your accent is foreign. That day might come.]

**ELHAM.**  Mamnoonam, Marjan joon.

Roozet bekher.

[Thank you, Marjan.

Have a good day.]

**MARJAN.**  Biya sar bezan.

[Don't be a stranger.]

**ELHAM.**  Inshallah.

[God willing.]

(**ELHAM** *leaves.*)

(**MARJAN** *erases the chalkboard.*)

## End of Play